WESTCHESTER PUBLIC LIBRARY

P9-DJK-552

Brands We Know

Nickelodeon

By Sara Green

Bellwether Media • Minneapolis, MN

Jump into the cockpit and take flight with Pilot books. Your journey will take you on high-energy adventures as you learn about all that is wild, weird, fascinating, and fun!

This is not an official Nickelodeon book. It is not approved by or connected with Nickelodeon or Viacom.

This edition first published in 2017 by Bellwether Media, Inc.

No part of this publication may be reproduced in whole or in part without written permission of the publisher.
For information regarding permission, write to Bellwether Media, Inc., Attention: Permissions Department,
5357 Penn Avenue South, Minneapolis, MN 55419.

Library of Congress Cataloging-in-Publication Data

Names: Green, Sara, 1964- author.
Title: Nickelodeon / by Sara Green.
Description: Minneapolis, MN : Bellwether Media, Inc., 2017. | Series:
Pilot: Brands We Know | Includes bibliographical references and index.
Identifiers: LCCN 2015043705 | ISBN 9781626174115 (hardcover : alk.
paper)
Subjects: LCSH: Nickelodeon (Television network)--Juvenile literature.
|Children's television programs--United States--Juvenile literature.
Classification: LCC PN1992.92.N55 G84 2017 | DDC 384.5506/5--dc23
LC record available at http://lccn.loc.gov/2015043705

Text copyright © 2017 by Bellwether Media, Inc. PILOT and associated logos are trademarks and/or registered trademarks of Bellwether Media, Inc. SCHOLASTIC, CHILDREN'S PRESS, and associated logos are trademarks and/or registered trademarks of Scholastic Inc.

Printed in the United States of America, North Mankato, MN.

nickelodeon

Table of Contents

What Is Nickelodeon?

The kids want an afternoon break after a long day at school. They decide to rest on the couch and watch a cartoon. They flip through the channels and stop on a colorful show. *SpongeBob SquarePants* is on Nickelodeon! The kids sit back and enjoy watching SpongeBob and his friends in Bikini Bottom.

Nickelodeon is an American cable television **network** that began in 1977. Many people shorten its name to Nick. The network is best known for its children's programs. It delights viewers with shows such as the *The Fairly OddParents* and *iCarly*. *Henry Danger*, *Game Shakers*, and *Sanjay and Craig* are recent fan favorites. Nick also makes movies, online games, and **apps**. A big company called Viacom owns Nickelodeon. Its **headquarters** is in New York City. However, Nick's programs are created in Burbank, California. Nick's bright orange **logo** is recognized around the world. Today, the network ranks among the top entertainment **brands** for kids!

By the Numbers

20
years in a row as the top-rated basic cable network

1
minute record for longest sliming ever

more than
158
countries that air Nickelodeon

more than
$12 billion
in sales from SpongeBob SquarePants merchandise

more than
100 million
U.S. households with the Nickelodeon channel

Nickelodeon Animation Studios

A New Network

A network called Pinwheel aired educational shows for children in 1977. Two years later, the network was renamed Nickelodeon. Soon, it began to air a popular **comedy** show called *You Can't Do That On Television*. The show dumped green slime on people. This happened whenever someone said, "I don't know." Audiences loved the slime. Nick began to use it in other shows. It became the brand's **trademark**!

The First Kids' Network
1980s tagline

Double Dare

The network's slimy shows were successful. But it still had low ratings in the early 1980s. Nick began to air commercials in 1983 to earn money. It focused more on entertainment kids would enjoy. Game shows like *Double Dare* became very popular. These changes paid off. Nickelodeon soon became the top-rated children's television station in the United States.

Would You Eat That?
Cottage cheese, vanilla pudding, and oatmeal have been used to make slime.

Nicktoons

Nickelodeon began to air original cartoons in 1991. The company named them Nicktoons. *Doug*, *Rugrats*, and *The Ren & Stimpy Show* were the first to air. They were huge hits. Soon, the network was getting more daily views than any other U.S. cable channel.

An **animator** named Jim Jinkins created *Doug*. He first wrote a book called *Doug Got a New Pair of Shoes*. Nick then turned it into a series. Arlene Klasky and Gábor Csupó made *Rugrats*. They modeled the kids in the show after their two sons. *The Ren & Stimpy Show* was created by John Kricfalusi. The series was **controversial**. Some parents thought the show was too **violent**. Still, many kids and adults loved John's silly characters.

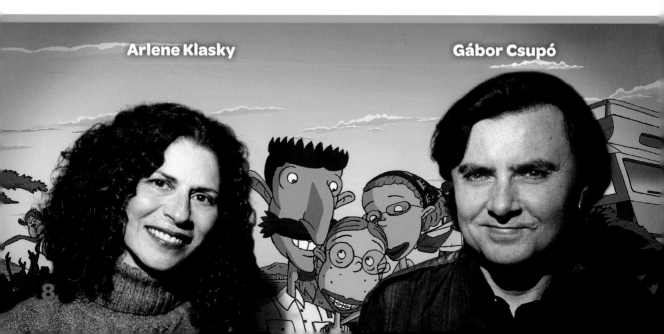

Arlene Klasky

Gábor Csupó

8

Favorite Nicktoons

Show	Air Date
Doug	1991
The Ren & Stimpy Show	1991
Rugrats	1991
Rocko's Modern Life	1993
Hey Arnold!	1996
KaBlam!	1996
The Wild Thornberrys	1998
SpongeBob SquarePants	1999
The Fairly OddParents	2001
Rabbids Invasion	2013
Sanjay and Craig	2013
Pig Goat Banana Cricket	2015
The Loud House	2016

For more than fifteen years, *The Fairly OddParents* and *SpongeBob SquarePants* have captured the hearts of many viewers. These shows came from creative minds. Butch Hartman developed *The Fairly OddParents*. He wanted to draw a character that could easily travel. He decided to include magic in the cartoon. Soon, Timmy Turner and his fairy friends were born. The show won an **Emmy** award in 2005. It also inspired three **live-action** movies.

Butch Hartman

Not Just Cartoons, We're Nicktoons
2000s tagline

10

A Spongy Name

SpongeBob SquarePants was originally called *SpongeBoy Ahoy!* The name changed because a mop was already called SpongeBoy.

Stephen Hillenburg created *SpongeBob SquarePants*. He first worked as a **marine biologist**. In time, Stephen returned to school to study animation. He then worked on a Nick show called *Rocko's Modern Life*. Soon, he drew a character that reminded him of his first job. But the character looked like a kitchen sponge instead of an ocean sponge. Stephen did not want people to think he drew cheese. He named the character SpongeBob SquarePants. The *SpongeBob SquarePants* show first aired in 1999. It quickly became one of Nickelodeon's top series. Today, SpongeBob **merchandise** is sold around the world.

Stephen Hillenburg

The Audience Grows

Nickelodeon reached a wider audience with more programs and shows. SNICK was launched in 1992. This Saturday night block of programs was aimed at preteens and teens. It included the shows *Are You Afraid of the Dark?* and *Kenan & Kel*. A comedy series called *All That* was another favorite. These shows drew many viewers. The network also launched other related channels in the late 1990s and early 2000s. Nickelodeon Games and Sports for Kids came out. A channel called Nicktoons was made just to air Nick's cartoons.

Kenan Thompson and Kel Mitchell of *Kenan & Kel*

Nick also made channels aimed at specific audiences. Noggin aired preschool shows like *Dora the Explorer*. In the evening, Noggin switched to become the N. It aired shows for teens. In 2009, Noggin became Nick Jr. and the N was renamed TeenNick. That same year, Nick changed its orange splat logo that could change shape. The network wanted a new logo that was similar across all its channels.

. . . .

Orange Splat
The orange splat is Nick's most famous logo. It was used for more than 25 years!

Nickelodeon's television schedule added The Splat in 2015. This block of programs airs each night on TeenNick. The Splat has reruns of popular shows from the 1990s through the early 2000s. *Legends of the Hidden Temple*, *Hey Arnold!*, and other favorites are back.

Since 1988, Nick has also aired the Kids' Choice Awards each year. Viewers choose their favorite television shows, actors, and movies. Winners receive an orange **blimp** award. The Kids' Choice Sports Awards started in 2014. Kids vote for their favorite athletes and sports moments. Winners of both award shows must pay attention on stage. Some get hit with green or gold slime!

Nick is Kids

1990s tagline

Nickelodeon Universe

Nickelodeon Universe is the largest indoor family theme park in the United States! People can see their favorite characters and enjoy many Nick-themed rides.

Box Office Hits

Nickelodeon began making children's movies in 1995. Its first movie, *Harriet the Spy*, was a **box office** success. More hits followed. *The Rugrats Movie* in 1998 made more than $100 million. Two years later, *Rugrats in Paris: The Movie* was also successful. SpongeBob and his friends are also movie stars. *The SpongeBob SquarePants Movie* made a splash in 2004. SpongeBob's next hit was a 3D adventure called *The SpongeBob Movie: Sponge Out of Water*. This movie combined live action with animation.

In 2012, *Rango* won an **Academy Award**. This animated movie is about a chameleon in the Old West. The 2014 movie *Teenage Mutant Ninja Turtles* made nearly $500 million worldwide. It was Nick's highest-earning movie ever!

. . . .

What Did You Call Me?

Johnny Depp voiced the character Rango. He said his kids called him the Lizard King during that time.

Healthy Kids, Healthy Earth

Nickelodeon helps people get fit and have fun. On the Worldwide Day of Play, the network stops all **broadcasts** for three hours. Nick encourages kids to be active instead of watching television or playing computer games. Many communities host Day of Play events. Kids enjoy launching slime and racing bikes.

Nick helps in other ways. Its Get Dirty Challenge inspires kids to protect the environment. There are many ways to take part. Kids can clean beaches, plant gardens, and teach others about wildlife. Jaheem Toombs, Erika Tham, and other stars lend a hand. They get dirty to protect the Earth. Nickelodeon connects with kids through entertainment and education!

Bee A Coder

Nickelodeon's "Bee A Coder" program teaches kids how to write computer code. Kids can use these skills to create their own computer games.

Nick stars Paola Andino and Nick Merico slime former NFL player Lousaka Polite to promote the Worldwide Day of Play

Nickelodeon Timeline

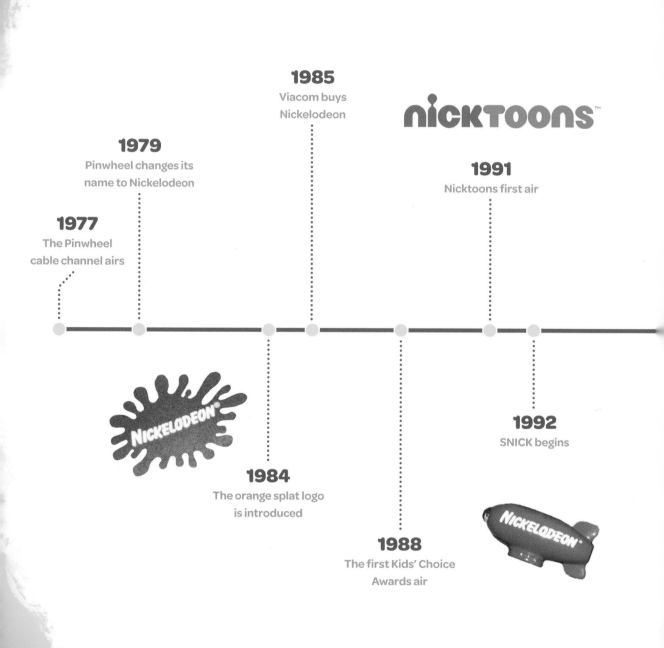

1985
Viacom buys
Nickelodeon

1979
Pinwheel changes its
name to Nickelodeon

1991
Nicktoons first air

1977
The Pinwheel
cable channel airs

1992
SNICK begins

1984
The orange splat logo
is introduced

1988
The first Kids' Choice
Awards air

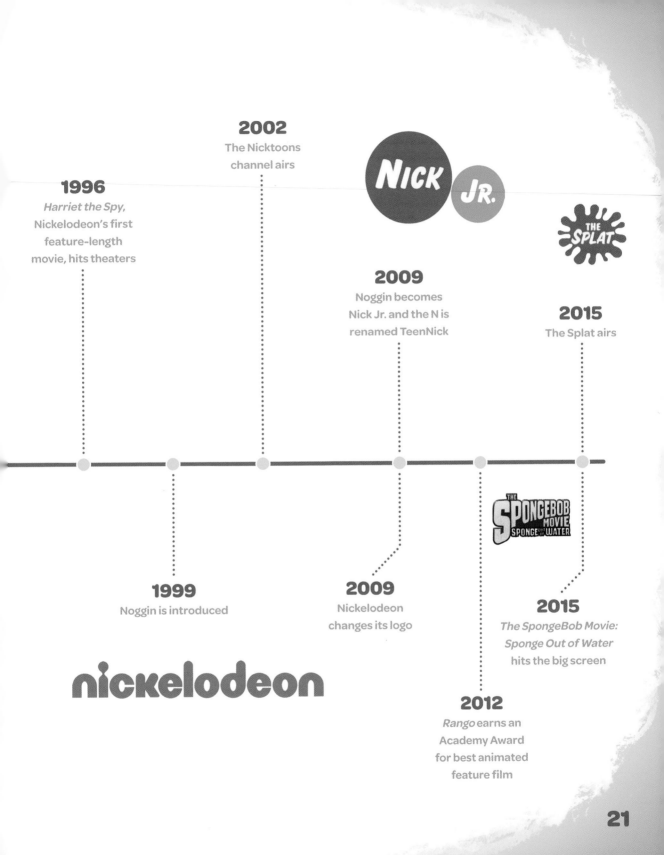

2002
The Nicktoons
channel airs

1996
Harriet the Spy,
Nickelodeon's first
feature-length
movie, hits theaters

2009
Noggin becomes
Nick Jr. and the N is
renamed TeenNick

2015
The Splat airs

1999
Noggin is introduced

2009
Nickelodeon
changes its logo

2015
*The SpongeBob Movie:
Sponge Out of Water*
hits the big screen

2012
Rango earns an
Academy Award
for best animated
feature film

Glossary

Academy Award—a yearly award presented for achievement in film; an Academy Award is also called an Oscar.

animator—an artist who works in animation; animation is created by a series of drawings that appear to move when shown very quickly, one after the other.

apps—small, specialized programs downloaded onto smartphones and other mobile devices

blimp—an airship that is filled with gas to float like a balloon

box office—a measure of ticket sales sold by a film or other performance

brands—categories of products all made by the same company

broadcasts—radio or television programs

comedy—entertainment that makes an audience laugh

controversial—causing a lot of discussion and disagreement

Emmy—an award given to the best shows and actors in the American television industry

headquarters—a company's main office

live-action—films that are not made by animation; live-action movies feature human actors.

logo—a symbol or design that identifies a brand or product

marine biologist—a scientist who studies ocean life

merchandise—items sold in a store

network—a television company that produces programs that people watch

trademark—an image, symbol, or word that distinguishes a company or product; trademarks are often legally protected so that other companies cannot use them.

violent—using physical force to cause harm

To Learn More

AT THE LIBRARY

Green, Sara. *Disney*. Minneapolis, Minn.: Bellwether Media, 2015.

Hunter, Nick. *Showtime!: The Entertainment Industry*. New York, N.Y.: Gareth Stevens Pub., 2013.

Walter Foster Creative Team. *Learn to Draw the Best of Nickelodeon*. Irvine, Calif.: Walter Foster, 2014.

ON THE WEB

Learning more about Nickelodeon is as easy as 1, 2, 3.

1. Go to www.factsurfer.com.

2. Enter "Nickelodeon" into the search box.

3. Click the "Surf" button and you will see a list of related web sites.

With factsurfer.com, finding more information is just a click away.

Index

The images in this book are reproduced through the courtesy of: Bojan Zivkovic, front cover (SpongeBob SquarePants); Bashutskyy, front cover (slime); Tinseltown, front cover (blimp); A.F. ARCHIVE/ Alamy, front cover (Dora and Boots, Hey Arnold!), pp. 8 (bottom), 10 (bottom), 11 (top left), 13 (bottom), 16 (top), 17 (top); Josh Brink, front cover (Rugrats, Fairly OddParents, Wild Thornberries, Nickeloden splat logo, Doug); Komarov Nickolay/ Wikipedia, table of contents, p. 21 (bottom middle); PARAMOUNT PICTURES/ SuperStock, pp. 4, 17 (bottom right); Junkyardsparkle/ Wikipedia, p. 5 (building); mexrix, p. 5 (sky); Christopher Polk/ KCA2016/ Getty Images, p. 6; Susan Aimee Weinik/ Getty Images, p. 7 (top); Jackie Brown/ Newscom, p. 7 (bottom); brink, pp. 9 (all), 11 (top right), 20 (bottom left); Gage Skidmore/ Wikipedia, p. 10 (top); Thardin12/ Wikipedia, p. 11 (top right); LAN/ Corbis, p. 11 (bottom); Jane Caine/ ZUMA Press, p. 12; JEAN-MARC BOUJU/ Alternative Press, p. 13 (top); Matt Sayles/ Alternative Press, p. 14 (bottom right); Dual Partition/ Wikipedia, pp. 14 (bottom left), 21 (top right); Jeffrey J Coleman, p. 15; Scott Legato/ Getty Images, p. 18; John Parra/ Getty Images, p. 19; Slrkn54/ Wikipedia, p. 20 (top right); Featureflash Photo Agency, p. 20 (bottom right); Duque Santiago/ Wikipedia, p. 21 (top right); EEIM, p. 21 (bottom).